£6.75

DATE DUE

GAYLORD			PRINTED IN U.S.A.

TENTH EDITION
TOTALLY REVISED AND
FULLY UPDATED

THE ESSENTIAL
EVENT
PLANNING KIT

A074169

THE ESSENTIAL EVENT PLANNING KIT

Godfrey Harris

THE AMERICAS GROUP
520 S. Selpulveda Blvd., Suite 204
Los Angeles, CA 90049 USA

FIRST EDITION	1st Printing—October 2001
SECOND EDITION	1st Printing—November 2001
	2nd Printing—March 2002
THIRD EDITION	May 2002
FOURTH EDITION	December 2002
FIFTH EDITION	November 2003
SIXTH EDITION	October 2004
SEVENTH EDITION	1st Printing—May 2005
	2nd Printing—November 2005
EIGHTH EDITION	August 2007
	2nd Printing—November 2005
NINTH EDITION	October 2009
TENTH EDITION	June 2011

The Americas Group
520 S. Sepulveda Blvd., Suite 204
Los Angeles, California 90049-3534
U.S.A.

☎	+ (1) 310 476 6374
FX	+ (1) 310 471 3276
EM	hrmg@mac.com
WWW	AMERICASGROUP.COM

ISBN:
0-935047-36-0

Library of Congress Cataloging-in-Publication Data

Harris, Godfrey, 1937-

  The essential event planning kit / Godfrey Harris.
      p. cm.
  ISBN 0-935047-36-0 (alk. paper)
   1. Special events--Planning. I. Title
  GT3405 .H37 2002
  394.2'068--dc21

                                                        2001053544

Printed in India by
Aegean Offset Printers, New Delhi

CONTENTS OF THE ESSENTIAL EVENT PLANNING KIT

Event Planning Notes — 7

Event Activities — EPK FORM A — 11

Planning Calendars — EPK FORMS B1 and B2 — 15

Fund Raising and Sponsorships — EPK FORM C — 19

Layout Map — EPK FORM D — 23

Furnishings — EPK FORM E — 27

Event Budget — EPK FORM F — 31

Planning Guide — EPK FORM G — 35

Event Checklist — EPK FORM H — 39

Event Program — EPK FORM I — 43

Contingency Considerations — EPK FORM J — 47

Event Goal and Evaluation — EPK FORMS K1 and K2 — 51

Sample Completed Forms — 55

Title Page for Completed EPK Forms to be Retained — 56

Thoughts / Ideas / Concerns — 57

Index — 58

About the Creator of The Essential Event Planning Kit — 60

DEDICATED TO

everyone
willing to take the time
and make the effort
to plan the details
that make events both
meaningful and memorable.

Godfrey Harris
Los Angeles, California
April 2011

EVENT PLANNING NOTES

EVENT PLANNING NOTES

Creating meaningful and memorable events always *seems* more daunting than it actually is. If those who plan events follow the hints in these notes and use the forms in this book, they will be surprised at how organized they become and how confident they feel during the planning and implementatiuon process. Best of all, they are likely to enjoy the event itself as much as their guests.

There are three cardinal **RULES** to follow in creating a successful event:

1. **Relax! Don't try to *think* of everything that needs to be done at once. Start by dividing the event into its major components.**
2. **Relax! Don't try to *remember* everything that needs attention. Jot notes as thoughts come to you.**
3. **Relax! Don't try to *accomplish* everything yourself. Let others help by working with you.**

Most planning begins with an idea of what you want to do at the event — honor an individual, bring a group together, conduct a ceremony. Even though you know where matters stand now and you have the end result well in mind, what is missing and what requires planning is resolving the details in between. This might involve selecting:

- VENUES
- INVITATIONS
- DECORATIONS
- REFRESHMENTS

- FAVORS
- ENTERTAINMENT
- SPEAKERS
- AMENITIES.

Event planning, then, is about the creation of a step-by-step process to get you from where you are to where you want to be. If you have a good sense of the resources at your disposal, moving from here to there only needs some orderly thought and reasoned consideration. *The Essential Event Planning Kit* is designed to help. And the starting point is determining the general theme of the event — or the atmosphere you want to generate. Once you have that in mind, obtain fixed commitments for the following crucial elements of any event:

- The best calendar DATE for the event and/or preferred DAY of the week.
- The precise SITE or best LOCATION for the event.
- The attendance of the PRINCIPAL GUEST(s) and/or KEY ATTRACTION(s) for the event.
- The amount you can afford to SPEND on the event.

All of the entries in the ESSENTIAL PLANNING KIT series — *The Essential Cooking Planning Kit, The Essential Diet Planning Kit, The Essential Gift Planning Kit, The Essential Moving Planning Kit, The Essential Project Planning Kit, The Essential Travel Planning Kit,* and *The Essential Wedding Planning Kit* — are grounded in the same philosophy: that PLANNING is as useful and necessary for individuals as it is for government agencies, nonprofit groups, and private businesses. Planning by individuals can prove to be both easy — when using the specially designed forms we have developed — *and* fun — when the planning process follows a logical path from start to finish.

Not all the forms presented in this book will prove useful or necessary to every reader for every event; some of the entries may not make sense for a particular situation. That's fine. Nowhere is it written that all of our forms have to be employed or that all spaces on each form have to be completed. Use what you want; forget the rest as you see fit. Remember also that there are no restrictions on making as many copies of the various forms in *The Essential Event Planning Kit* as may be needed. In fact, since we advise planners to draft and redraft their plans as new circumstances dictate, as new ideas arise, and as collateral decisions are reached, the best planners seem to be the most active with the photocopying equipment. It is a good idea that each time you revise a form, you give each version a consecutive number and the date on which it was written or revised to keep track of the changes.

Another thought. Professional golfers are known to retain the notes they make on every hole on every course they play throughout their careers. Such matters as prevailing winds, distances, sight lines, hole locations, hazards, ridges, slopes and other factors prove invaluable on every subsequent round played on the same course. We recommend that you keep all the forms you make for each event you plan for future reference should you want to repeat something or should you want to share your knowledge with others. A title page for these retained forms is on page 56.

You should know that your event is a large part of a nation's annual activities. In the United States, most people attend some 24 events a year — birthdays, anniversaries, holidays, weddings, commemorations, receptions, openings, parties, etc. — that someone has carefully planned and prepared. Take the Super Bowl. Each year more than 100 million Americans gather to watch this annual football game to decide the national professional championship; more than ten million man-hours are devoted to making the arrangements and preparing the food for this event alone.

Finally, you should know that the need for advance planning for every undertaking is not shared by everyone. Some refuse to review their assumptions or acknowledge the possibility of change. Take a Senator's aide who recently argued with a Washington, DC travel agent about the need for getting his boss a visa before leaving on a trip for China. "Look," said the aide, "I've been there four times myself and they've accepted my American Express every time." The moral of the story is that change happens. Good planning makes dealing with change easier.

EVENT ACTIVITIES

FORM A

EVENT ACTIVITIES

Start a separate **EVENT ACTIVITIES FORM** — EPK FORM A — for each MAJOR ELEMENT of the event — decorations, entertainment, guests, and so forth. The COMPONENTS of each MAJOR ELEMENT are such matters as themes, music, names, and a lot more.

Put ideas, questions, and notes in the THOUGHTS column as they occur to you. Treat your first ideas on each MAJOR ELEMENT as rough notes. For example, you might title one of the sheets INVITATIONS to begin thinking through the details involved in creating and delivering the invitations: Ideas on components such as wording, style and/or material to be used, a printer and/or calligrapher to be located, the amount of time to leave between mailing the invitations and the event itself, and so on.

In the THOUGHTS column alongside each of these COMPONENTS, jot down whatever ideas come to you. Opposite "Wording," for example, you might put reminders of things that need to be decided:

- Should *responses* be handled by phone, EMail, or snail mail? If EMail, what address should be used? If phone, who might be designated to receive the calls?
- Should there be a recommended dress code? How will it be described?
- What time should the event start and end?

The latter two points—occurring in the course of thinking through questions concerning the invitation—are a good example of how each *element* of an event forces consideration about other elements that might have forgotten or ignored.

EVENT
ACTIVITIES

VERSION #_____

MAJOR ELEMENT

EVENT
ACTIVITIES

_____/_____/_____ **DATE**

COMPONENTS	THOUGHTS

PHOTOCOPYING ENCOURAGED

EPK **FORM A**

PLANNING CALENDARS

FORMS B1 AND B2

PLANNING CALENDARS

Create a **PLANNING CALENDAR** for the period of time between now and the event itself. Use either the **MONTHLY CALENDAR** — EPK FORM B1 on page 17 — or the **ANNUAL CALENDAR** — EPK FORM B2 on the next page — to create a schedule of activities that encompasses the scope of your event.

Enter the appropriate date against each day in the month on EPK FORM B1 or the dates of the Monday to Friday dates for each week of the month on EPK FORM B2. When a month has say five Mondays or five Thursdays, instead of the normal four, draw a diagonal line through the box from Northeast to Southwest to accommodate all the days in a full month.

In filling in the boxes, it is sometimes easier to put ending dates for each activity first and work back to the starting date (e.g., the date invitations are to be mailed, the date the invitation master is to be delivered to the printer, the date the wording needs to be approved, and so on.)

MONTHLY CALENDAR

VERSION #____

MONTHLY CALENDAR

____/____/____ **DATE**

SUNDAY		MONDAY		TUESDAY		WEDNESDAY	THURSDAY		FRIDAY		SATURDAY	
SUNDAY		MONDAY		TUESDAY		WEDNESDAY	THURSDAY		FRIDAY		SATURDAY	
SUNDAY		MONDAY		TUESDAY		WEDNESDAY	THURSDAY		FRIDAY		SATURDAY	
SUNDAY		MONDAY		TUESDAY		WEDNESDAY	THURSDAY		FRIDAY		SATURDAY	
SUNDAY		MONDAY		TUESDAY		WEDNESDAY	THURSDAY		FRIDAY		SATURDAY	

PHOTOCOPYING ENCOURAGED

EPK **FORM B1**

ANNUAL CALENDAR

VERSION #____

ANNUAL CALENDAR

YEAR

	JAN	FEB	MAR	APR	MAY	JUN	JUL	AUG	SEP	OCT	NOV	DEC
WEEK 1	____TO____	____TO____	____TO____	____TO____	____TO____	____TO____	____TO____	____TO____	____TO____	____TO____	____TO____	____TO____
WEEK 2	____TO____	____TO____	____TO____	____TO____	____TO____	____TO____	____TO____	____TO____	____TO____	____TO____	____TO____	____TO____
WEEK 3	____TO____	____TO____	____TO____	____TO____	____TO____	____TO____	____TO____	____TO____	____TO____	____TO____	____TO____	____TO____
WEEK 4	____TO____	____TO____	____TO____	____TO____	____TO____	____TO____	____TO____	____TO____	____TO____	____TO____	____TO____	____TO____
WEEK 5	____TO____	____TO____	____TO____	____TO____	____TO____	____TO____	____TO____	____TO____	____TO____	____TO____	____TO____	____TO____

PHOTOCOPYING ENCOURAGED

EPK **FORM B2**

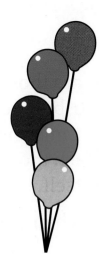

FUND RAISING AND SPONSORSHIPS

FORM C

FUND RAISING AND SPONSORSHIPS

If you need financial support for an event, the most likely sources of help are those closest to you. Start with family, friends, and associates. Ask them to contribute to or invest in your project, but only for an amount that they truly wouldn't miss or have no immediate need for. Move outward from those closest to you to reach those individuals or organizations with an affiliation to or affinity for the event itself.

Be realistic. Donations or contributions are usually made to support events when the *giver* can justify two values in terms of the cost involved:

- The benefit to the recipient getting the money; and
- The benefit to the donor providing the money.

Keep both factors in mind when you rehearse your oral pitch or draft your written proposal. Make sure to cover the purpose of the event; its importance to the community; its special features; the people, organizations, and/or institutions involved; how benefactors will receive credit for their participation; and the basis for your belief in the event's ultimate success. Make your pitch or your document something easily repeated or copied for those who will have to forward your request to others for approval.

FUND RAISING

FUND RAISING

IDENTIFY ELEMENT FOR SPONSORSHIP OR WHOLE EVENT

VERSION #_____

_____/_____/_____ DATE

CONTACT THIS PERSON	TO REACH THIS POTENTIAL SOURCE	FOR THIS TYPE OF DONATION		FOR THIS PERCEIVED BENEFIT
		ITEM	$	
		ITEM	$	
		ITEM	$	
		ITEM	$	
		ITEM	$	
		ITEM	$	
		ITEM	$	
		ITEM	$	
		ITEM	$	
		ITEM	$	
		ITEM	$	
		ITEM	$	

PHOTOCOPYING ENCOURAGED

EPK FORM C

LAYOUT MAP

FORM D

LAYOUT MAP

Create a "blueprint" of the venue(s) to be used for your event on the **LAYOUT MAP** — EPK FORM D — or use a larger piece of paper for the same purpose. Determine the actual size and shape of the venue(s) where the principal activities will take place.

The grid on EPK FORM D consists of 15 horizontal and 10 vertical squares. Draw a rough outline around the squares in the shape of the space you will use. Let each square represent an actual on-the-ground measurement (representing so many feet or meters) to allow you to get an approximate idea of how everything will be arranged and spaced.

Trace or cutout as many shapes as needed from EPK FORM E to make trial arrangements of the tables, chairs, and ancilliary equipment. Remember that you are working with estimated size and distances; precise placements will have to wait until you are on the ground. Be sure to leave sufficient room for the movement of people (including those in wheelchairs, with walkers, or needing other forms of assistance) and plan sites for such traditional aspects of an event as a registration desk, podium, refreshment center, back-of-the-room sales area, and so on. If more than one room or space is involved in an event, make as many duplicates of the Layout Map as needed.

LAYOUT MAP

VERSION #_____

ROOM/LOCATION NAME

LAYOUT MAP

_____/_____/_____ **DATE**

PHOTOCOPYING ENCOURAGED

EPK **FORM D**

FURNISHINGS

FORM E

FURNISHINGS

After making as many photocopies of **FURNISHINGS** — EPK FORM E — as needed, trace or cut out the table shape(s) or seating pattern(s) that will be used at the event to handle guests, presentations, and/or serving areas. Do the same with the ancilliary equipment to be placed on the floor.

If your event involves rows of seats arranged in auditorium style, determine the allowable number in each row as well as the proper width of the aisle(s) from the venue manager and/or the fire department before creating any seating blocks. Remember that it is infinitely easier to be in compliance with all the rules and fulfill all the needs of an event when you move and adjust furniture and decorations on paper rather than having to shift the actual furniture and equipment on the ground.

Some standard sizes and typical spacings may help you plan your event:

- Seats: 16" (40cm) wide. In auditorium seating, leave 18" (46cm) between back of seat in one row and front of seat in the next row.

- Tables: 72" (183cm) in diameter for 12 people; 60" (152cm) for 10 people; 52" (132cm) for 8 people; 48" (122cm) for 6 people; and 36" (92cm) for 4 people.

- Aisle widths or table spacing: 36" (92cm) between the edges of objects.

FURNISHINGS

SCREEN   OVERHEAD   MICROPHONES

LIGHTS   LECTURN

TABLE
SIZES/SHAPES

SPEAKERS   HEATERS

(10)

(4)

FANS

(8)

(6)

COAT RACKS

EASELS   PLANTS

AISLES

(4)

AUDITORIUM SEATING
CONFIGURATIONS

(8)

(2)

PHOTOCOPYING ENCOURAGED

EVENT BUDGET

FORM F

EVENT BUDGET

Building an **EVENT BUDGET** — EPK FORM F — is like constructing a house — every aspect of the construction from the concrete in the foundation to the shingles on the roof have a specific cost with the value of each dependent on both the quality and the quantity involved.

Just as an architect sketches out a concept before continually refining the elements into an affordable and pleasing structure, so those who plan events need to work from an overall vision of the event before trying to find the right balance of design and ingredients to insure both affordability and memorability.

When costs are not known, make your best guess and refine them as additional information becomes available.

EVENT BUDGET

VERSION #_____

IDENTIFY MAJOR ELEMENT OR WHOLE EVENT

EVENT BUDGET

_____/_____/_____ **DATE**

THIS ACTIVITY	WITH THESE COMPONENTS	AT THIS UNIT COST		THIS NUMBER OF UNITS		THIS TOTAL AMOUNT
			X		=	$
			X		=	$
			X		=	$
			X		=	$
			X		=	$
			X		=	$
			X		=	$
			X		=	$
			X		=	$
			X		=	$
			X		=	$
		TOTAL			=	$

PHOTOCOPYING ENCOURAGED

EPK **FORM F**

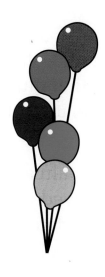

PLANNING GUIDE

FORM G

PLANNING GUIDE

Because the **PLANNING CALENDAR** — EPK FORM B —can become too cluttered, start building a **PLANNING GUIDE.** It allows you to record the smallest detail that must be accomplished along with the date and/or time of its expected completion, its cost, and the person charged with accomplishing it.

As you work through this form, you may have to go back to change dates already entered on the **PLANNING CALENDAR.** For example, you may have allowed two weeks to address the invitations. Working backwards, you may find that the date inadvertently selected to pick up the invitations is the Friday start of a three-day holiday when traffic may be heavy or the print shop may close early. As a result, you would want to add a few days to this part of the schedule. The more refined your thinking becomes to deal with challenges and the unexpected, the more organized you will be and the more relaxed you will feel.

PLANNING GUIDE

IDENTIFY COMPONENT

PLANNING GUIDE

VERSION #_____

____/____/____ **DATE**

ACCOMPLISH THIS TASK	WITH THIS PERSON'S HELP	BY THIS DATE/TIME	AT THIS COST	DONE?

PHOTOCOPYING ENCOURAGED

EPK **FORM G**

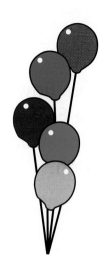

EVENT CHECKLIST

FORM H

EVENT CHECKLIST

All the activities that must come together on the day of the event itself — from flower delivery to catering to transporting the principals — should be listed on the **EVENT CHECKLIST** — EPK FORM H — along with the name of persons responsible for seeing that the items or individuals get to the event site from their pre-event location.

EVENT
CHECKLIST

VERSION #_____

IDENTIFY SEPARATE ELEMENTS OF EVENT

EVENT
CHECKLIST

_____/_____/_____ DATE

√	ITEM	LOCATION	RESPONSIBILITY	√	ITEM	LOCATION	RESPONSIBILITY

PHOTOCOPYING ENCOURAGED

EPK FORM H

EVENT PROGRAM

FORM I

EVENT PROGRAM

Every activity that is planned for the event itself should be noted on the **EVENT PRO-GRAM** — EPK FORM I — to ensure that the entire effort runs smoothly.

This form should be used and refined after rehearsals or following a verbal "walk through" of the event with other participants. Don't guess. Time each activity with a watch and make sure to leave mandatory catch-up periods for unavoidable delays and unexpected occurrences.

Rehearse every aspect of the program. Think through who should make announcements and when they should be made. Check sound levels to make sure conversations are not overwhelmed by a band, DJ, or adjacent activities.

EVENT PROGRAM

VERSION #_____

EVENT TITLE

EVENT PROGRAM

_____/_____/_____ **DATE**

AT THIS TIME	THIS ACTIVITY OCCURS	INVOLVING THIS DETAIL
____:____ __M		
____:____ __M		
____:____ __M		
____:____ __M		
____:____ __M		
____:____ __M		
____:____ __M		
____:____ __M		
____:____ __M		
____:____ __M		
____:____ __M		
____:____ __M		
____:____ __M		
____:____ __M		
____:____ __M		
____:____ __M		
____:____ __M		
____:____ __M		
____:____ __M		

PHOTOCOPYING ENCOURAGED

EPK **FORM I**

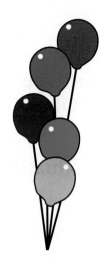

CONTINGENCY CONSIDERATIONS

FORM J

CONTINGENCY CONSIDERATIONS

List the possible and potential problems that might befall a principal, the type of adverse weather that might occur for the area or season of the event, and the type of emergencies that have happened in the recent past on **CONTINGENCY CONSID-ERATIONS** — EPK FORM J.

For each contingency listed, note what action might be taken to ameliorate a situation and how that action might affect the site, the timing, and/or the guests.

You need not be precise in your descriptions or your potential adjustment to a perceived problem. It is enough at this stage to consider a few options or maneuvers that might be employed should a problem actually occur. As a particular contingency becomes more imminent, you can refine your adjustments and/or solutions.

We would amend an old Massachusetts Mutual Insurance Company slogan this way: *You can't predict, but you can prepare.*

CONTINGENCY CONSIDERATIONS

VERSION #_____

CONTINGENCY CONSIDERATIONS

____/____/____ **DATE**

EVENT TITLE

TYPE OF CONCERN	IF THIS OCCURS... (DESCRIBE BRIEFLY)	POSSIBLE CHANGES IN SITE/TIMING	POTENTIAL IMPACT ON GUESTS
PROBLEM BEFALLING A PRINCIPAL			
ECONOMIC/FINANCIAL COMPLICATIONS			
WEATHER FACTORS			
POTENTIAL NATURAL DISASTER			
ACCIDENT OR OTHER EMERGENCY OCCURENCE			
POLICE/LABOR ACTIONS			

PHOTOCOPYING ENCOURAGED

EPK **FORM J**

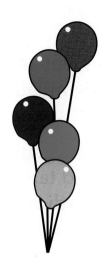

EVENT GOAL AND EVALUATION

FORMS K1 AND K2

EVENT GOAL AND EVALUATION

We see planning a little differently than others. We believe that the goal statement—EPK FORM K—should be formalized only *after* all the planning steps have been contemplated and the major arrangements have been considered.

We believe this makes the goal statement much more realistic, encouraging organizers to review plans and arrangements to insure that they meet their intended target. Political observers have come to realize that the political continuum from radical to reactionary is circular rather than linear (with little *real* difference between these two seeming extremes). By the same token, planning an event can end with a re-articulation of the goals to be achieved.

We also believe that you should evaluate an event immediately after it ends. Gather everyone's comments, as well as your own, for a hard-nosed assessment of what went right, what went wrong, and why. Don't wait. If you delay any length of time to review a just concluded event, you are likely to lose key details and perhaps be condemned to make the same mistakes again.

Justice Oliver Wendell Holmes, Jr., once famously noted that there is no good writing, only good *re-writing*. As a result, it isn't how you draft your original **EVENT GOAL** or your preliminary **EVALUATION** on EPK FORMS K1 AND K2 that counts, it's how close the final version comes to expressing your thoughts on what will make this event a success and what will make another event a more impressive success in the future.

EVENT
GOAL

VERSION #_____

EVENT TITLE

EVENT
GOAL

____ / ____ / ____ DATE

TO...

PHOTOCOPYING ENCOURAGED

EPK **FORM K1**

EVALUATION

ACTIVITY

EVALUATION

VERSION_____

____/____/____ DATE

THIS ASPECT	COULD HAVE BEEN IMPROVED BY	WITH ATTENTION TO THIS DETAIL

PHOTOCOPYING ENCOURAGED

EPK FORM K2

SAMPLE COMPLETED FORMS

EVENT ACTIVITIES

EVENT ACTIVITIES

VERSION 1

MAJOR ELEMENT: MEETING ROOM

05/11/01 DATE

COMPONENTS	THOUGHTS
REFRESHMENTS	COFFEE / TEA / COKE / DIET COKE / COOKIES DIET 7-UP / ↳ ENG. BREAKFAST / HERBAL
ROOM	U-SHAPED TABLE / DETACHED HEAD TABLE - BOOK SALE AREA
EQUIPMENT	OVERHEAD / EASLE OR CHALK BOARD / PORTABLE (LAPEL) MIKE
NAME PLAQUES	DO WE WANT? WHO WRITES NAMES? FIRST ONLY OR BOTH?

PHOTOCOPYING ENCOURAGED   EPK **FORM A**

EVENT BUDGET

EVENT BUDGET

VERSION 2

IDENTIFY MAJOR ELEMENT OR WHOLE EVENT: WOM SEMINAR

06/11/01 DATE

THIS ACTIVITY...	WITH THESE COMPONENTS...	AT THIS UNIT COST...	X	THIS NUMBER OF UNITS...	=	THIS TOTAL AMOUNT...
MAILINGS	LETTERS	$.65/PC	X	1000 PIECES	=	$650
	POSTCARDS	$.33/PC	X	1000 PIECES	=	$330
ADVERTISING	LA TIMES	$290/INCH	X	2 INSERTIONS	=	$580
	DAILY NEWS	$190/INCH	X	3 INSERTIONS	=	$570
MATERIALS	MANUAL	$2.25 EA	X	50 COPIES	=	$113
	CERTIFICATES	$1.00 EA	X	50	=	$50
	PRIZES	$1.00 EA	X	15 TICKETS	=	$15
HOTEL	ROOM	$100/HR	X	3 HOURS	=	$300
	REFRESH.	$1.50/HEAD	X	50	=	$75
	PARKING	$3.00/CAR	X	20 CARS	=	$60
CONTING.	—	12% OF SUB-TOTAL ($)	X	[$2473]	=	$297
				TOTAL	=	$2770

PHOTOCOPYING ENCOURAGED   EPK **FORM F**

PLANNING CALENDAR

PLANNING CALENDAR

VERSION 3

MONTH: JULY

05/15/01 DATE

SUNDAY	MONDAY	TUESDAY	WEDNESDAY	THURSDAY	FRIDAY	SATURDAY
1 RUN FINAL NEWSPAPER AD	2	3	4	5 MAIL SECOND POSTCARD TO LIST	6	7
8	9	10	11	12 MAKE REMINDER CALLS	13 MAKE REMINDER CALLS	14
15	16 CLOSE SEMINAR CREATE ROSTER	17 BOX MATERIALS	18 TAKE MATERIALS TO HOTEL	19 SEMINAR	20 CLEAN UP	21
22	23 ASSESSMENT LETTERS OUT	24	25	26	27	28
29	30	31				

PHOTOCOPYING ENCOURAGED   EPK **FORM B**

EVENT PROGRAM

EVENT PROGRAM

VERSION 3

EVENT TITLE: WOM SEMINAR

06/19/01 DATE

AT THIS TIME...	THIS ACTIVITY OCCURS...	UNDER THESE CONDITIONS...
12:00	DESIREE @ HOTEL	GETS ROOM OPEN
	PENNY @ HOTEL	SETS UP BOOK SALE
	JEFF @ HOME CHANGING	
1:00	JEFF ARRANGES SAMPLES / OVERHEADS / PRIZES	AT HOTEL
2:00	SEMINAR BEGINS	JEFF
3:15	BREAK TIME	BARBARA HOSTS
4:30	SEMINAR ENDS	CERTS AWARDED
5:00	DEPART HOTEL	ROOM CLOSED

PHOTOCOPYING ENCOURAGED   EPK **FORM I**

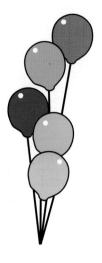

EVENT DATE

_____

EVENT DESIGNATION

NOTES/IDEAS/CONCERNS

INDEX

A

Accidents — 49
Action — 48
Activities — 16, 44
Addresses — 12
Adversity — 36
Affiliation — 20
Affinity — 20
Affordability — 32
Aisles — 24, 25
American Express — 10
Amenities — 9
Architect — 32
Arrangements — 24, 52
Associates — 30, 36
Assumptions — 10
Atmosphere — 9
Attractions — 9
Auditorium — 24, 25

B

Balance — 32
Band — 12, 44
Benfactors — 20
Beneficiaries — 20
Blocks — 24
Blueprint — 24
Budget — 32, 36
Buildings — 32

C

Calendar — 16
Calligraphers — 12
Ceremonies — 8
Chairs — 24

Change — 10, 52
Checkmark — 36
Checklist — 40
China — 10
Circumstances — 10
Clutter — 36
Coat racks — 25
Colors — 12
Commercial
  businesses — 9
Commitments — 9
Complications — 49
Components — 12, 32, 36
Concrete — 32
Conferences — 60
Confidence — 8
Consequences — 52
Construction — 32
Contingencies — 48
Contractors — 60
Contributions — 20
Coordination — 60
Costs — 32, 36
Cutouts — 24

D

Dates — 9, 16, 36
Days — 9, 16, 40
Decisions — 10
Decorations — 8, 12
Dedication — 6
Delays — 44, 52
Details — 36, 52
Diagonal line — 16

Dinners — 60
Diplomacy — 60
Disasters — 49
DJ — 44
Donations — 20
Done — 36
Drafts — 52
Dress code — 12

E

Easels — 25
Elements— 12, 32
Emergencies — 48, 49
Enjoyment — 8
Entertainment — 9, 12
Envelopes — 12
Equipment — 24
Essential Cooking Planning Kit, The — 9
Essential Diet Planning Kit, The — 9
Essential Gift Planning Kit, The — 9
Essential Moving Planning Kit, The — 9
Essential Project Planning Kit, The — 9
Essential Travel Planning Kit, The — 9
Essential Wedding Planning Kit, The— 9
Estimates — 32
Evaluation — 52
Event program — 44
Exhibits — 60

F

Family — 20
Fans — 25
Favors — 9
Financing — 20
Fire Department — 24
Five-day months —16
Flowers — 25
Foot — 24
Forgetfulness —
Forms — 8, 9
Foundation — 32
Four-day months —16
Friends — 12, 20
Fund raising — 20
Funerals — 60
Furnishings — 24

G

Goals — 52
Golfers — 10
Government — 9
Groups — 8
Guessing — 44
Guest list — 12
Guests — 12, 48, 60
Guide — 36

H

Harris, Godfrey — 6, 60
Harris/Ragan Management
  Group — 60
Heaters — 25

Help — 8
Holiday — 36
Holmes, Jr., Justice Oliver Wendell — 52
Hopes — 52
House — 32

I
Ideas — 10, 12
Illness — 24, 48
Inches — 20
Individuals — 8
Ingredients 32
Insurance — 48
Investments — 20
Invitations — 8, 12, 16, 36

K
Knowledge — 8

L
Labor — 49
Layout — 24
Lecturns — 25
Lights — 25
Linear — 52
Location — 9, 24, 40

M
Mail — 12, 16
Manager — 24
Map — 24
Massachusetts Mutal — 48
Material — 12
Measurements — 20
Meetings — 60
Memorable — 32
Meters – 24

Metric — 24
Microphones — 25
Milestones — 16
Millimeters – 24
Money — 9, 20
Months — 16

N
Nonprofits — 9
Notes — 8, 12

O
Orderly — 9
Organized — 8 , 36
Outline — 24
Overheads — 25

P
Paper — 24
Parties — 60
Philosophy — 9
Photocopying — 24
Planners — 8, 32, 52
Planning — 8, 10
Podium — 24
Police — 49
Predict — 48
Prepare — 48
Presentations — 20, 24
Principals — 48
Print shops — 12, 36
Printer — 12, 16
Problems — 48
Program — 44
Proposal — 20

Q
Questions — 12

R
Reactionary — 52
Reasoned — 9
Receptions — 10, 60
Recipients — 20
Redrafts — 10
Refreshments — 8, 24
Registrations — 24
Rehearsals — 20, 44
Relaxation — 8, 36
Remembering — 8
Resources — 9
Responses — 12
Responsibilities — 40
Re-writing — 52
Roof — 32
Rows—24
Rules — 24

S
Sales — 28
Samples — 55
Senate — 10
Schedule — 36
Screens — 25
Season — 48
Seating — 24
Seminars — 60
Serving areas — 24
Shapes — 16, 20, 24
Shingles — 32
Site — 9
Size — 16, 24
Sketches — 24, 32
Slogan — 48
Sound — 44
Spacing — 24, 28

Speakers — 9, 25
Sponsorship — 20
Stopwatch — 44
Structure — 32
Style — 12
Success — 52
Super Bowl — 10
Support — 20

T
Tables — 24
Telephone — 12
Themes — 9, 12
Thinking — 8
Thoughts — 12, 52
Timing — 12, 48
Trace — 24
Traffic — 36
Travel agent — 10
Trips — 10, 60

U
Unexpected — 44

V
Value — 20, 32
Venue — 8, 16, 20, 24
Version — 52
Visa — 10
Vision — 32

W
Washington, DC — 10
Weather — 48, 49
Word of mouth advertising — 60
Wording — 12
Writing — 52

ABOUT THE CREATOR OF THE ESSENTIAL EVENT PLANNING KIT

GODFREY HARRIS has been a public policy consultant based in Los Angeles, California, since 1968. He began consulting after serving as a university instructor at UCLA and Rutgers, a U.S. Army intelligence officer, a U.S. foreign service officer with the Department of State, an organizational specialist in President Lyndon Johnson's Executive Office, and as a program manager for an international financial company in Geneva.

In all of these positions, Harris honed his planning skills when he was called upon to organize or manage meetings, dinners, trips, exhibits, funerals, conferences, seminars, receptions, parties, and other diplomatic, social, and commercial events requiring coordinating the activities of colleagues, contractors, and guests. At present, he serves as Curator of the Da Vinci Exhibit, a museum-quality display of the machines, art, and philosophy of Leonardo da Vinci.

As President of Harris/Ragan Management Group, Harris has focused the firm's activities on projects that offer alternative solutions to matters of community concern. In fulfilling that role, he has specialized in political and economic analysis; marketing public and private sector services through word of mouth advertising; developing new environmental and commercial products; promoting international tourism to various destinations; and creating commemorative, enlightening, and educational events.

Harris has written on his own or with associates 60 other books. He holds degrees from Stanford University and the University of California, Los Angeles.

OTHER BOOKS BY GODFREY HARRIS

Courting Failure (with Kennith L Harris)
The Legacy of Leonardo da Vinci
Timeline — The Principal Events During the Lifetime of Leonardo da Vinci
Exhibit Catalog of the Da Vinci Experience —1st, 2nd, 3rd, 4th, & 5th Editions
Leonardo Quotebook
The Life and Contributions of Leonardo da Vinci (with Thomas Mankowski)
Coloring with Leonardo (with Daniel Mankowski)
What a Great Idea!
The Definitive Southern California Diet (with Jeffrey I. Barke, M.D.)
The Hottest Ideas in Word of Mouth Advertising
The Complete Business Guide
The Essential Gift Planning Kit
The Essential Diet Planning Kit (with Jeffrey I. Barke, M.D.)
The Essential Wedding Planning Kit
The Essential Cooking Planning Kit
The Essential Project Planning Kit
Civility
Corruption
The Essential Moving Planning Kit —1st, 2nd, & 3rd Editions (with Mike H. Sarbakhsh)
The Essential Travel Planning Kit —1st & 2nd Editions
Grandparenting
The Essential Event Planning Kit —1st, 2nd, 3rd, 4th, 5th, 6th, 7th, 8th, & 9th *Editions*
Watch It!
Concentration —1st & 2nd Editions (with Kennith L Harris)
Let Your Fingers Do the Talking
Talk Is Easy
The Ultimate Black Book —3rd Edition (with Kennith L Harris and Mark B Harris)
Don't Take Our Word for It!
How to Generate Word of Mouth Advertising (with Gregrey J Harris)
Promoting International Tourism —1st & 2nd Editions (with Kenneth M. Katz)
European Union Almanac —1st & 2nd Editions (with Hans J. Groll and Adelheid Hasenknopf)
The Panamanian Problem (with Guillermo de St. Malo A.)
Mapping Russia and Its Neighbors (with Sergei A. Diakonov)
Power Buying (with Gregrey J Harris)
Talk Is Cheap (with Gregrey J Harris)
The Fascination of Ivory
Invasion (with David S. Behar)
The Ultimate Black Book —2nd Edition (with Kennith L Harris)
The Ultimate Black Book
The Panamanian Perspective
Commercial Translations (with Charles Sonabend)
From Trash to Treasure (with Barbara DeKovner-Mayer)
Panama's Position
The Quest for Foreign Affairs Officers (with Francis Fielder)
The History of Sandy Hook, New Jersey
Outline of Social Sciences
Outline of Western Civilization